Nadim's mum and dad had to go away, so Nadim came to stay at Biff and Chip's house.

Nadim had a bag with all his things, but he had a big box, too.

"What's in that big box?" asked Chip.

"Wait and see," said Nadim.

The children went to Biff's room. Nadim had
the big box. He opened it and took out his
computer.

"Brilliant!" said Chip.

"I've got some new computer games," said
Nadim. "But we can play with them later. I've got
something else to play with."

Nadim had some robots.

"These are great," said Kipper. "I'm going to get one like this. It's my favourite."

Biff and Chip had a robot, too. They went to fetch it.

"We're going to have a great time," said Nadim.

Wilf came to play. He had one of his new toys.
It was a space craft.

Biff, Wilf and Kipper played with all the toys.
Kipper said he wanted to be a robot when he
grew up.

"You can't," said Biff. "People can't be robots."

Chip and Nadim played on the computer. One of Nadim's new games was called "Storm Castle". It looked exciting.

"It's quite hard," said Nadim. "I'll show you how to play, then you can have a go."

"It looks great," said Chip.

Everyone watched Nadim play Storm Castle.

"You have to go through all the rooms," he said.
"But there is a danger in every room. Look."

In the first room, the floor opened. You could
fall through, but Nadim didn't.

"That was clever," said Chip.

Nadim was good on the computer. He got through all the rooms safely.

"Chip can have a go next," said Nadim. "You can all have a go if you like."

"You're brilliant at it," said Chip. "I won't be very good when I have my go."

Suddenly, the magic key began to glow.

"Oh no!" said Biff. "I don't want the key to glow. I don't want a magic adventure. I want to play on Nadim's computer."

"I don't want a magic adventure, either," said Chip. "I think I know where it will be."

"Where do you think it will be?" asked Kipper.

"Storm Castle," said Chip.

"Oh no!" said Wilf. "I don't think we're going to like this adventure. Storm Castle is full of dangers."

"It's a good job Nadim is with us," said Biff.

The magic didn't take them inside the castle.
It took them to a desert. Storm Castle was in front
of them.

"Why didn't the magic take us inside the castle?"
said Wilf.

"And where's Nadim?" asked Chip.

"Oh no! Giant robots," said Wilf. "Run for it!"

The children ran as fast as they could. The robots were not very fast, but there were lots of them.

"We'll have to get into Storm Castle," said Biff. "Come on."

The children saw a bridge. It was the only way to the castle.

"This is the way in," said Wilf. "The robots can't get across this."

"I hope it's safe," said Chip. "It's a long way to fall."

Suddenly, the bridge began to open in the middle.

"Jump for it!" called Chip. "If it opens too much, you won't get across."

Biff and Kipper ran as fast as they could. Then they jumped across.

Wilf was still on the other side. The gap was getting wider and wider.

"Come on, Wilf!" called Biff. "You can do it. Run as fast as you can and jump. We'll grab you."

Wilf ran and jumped.

"Hooray! He's made it," shouted Kipper.

The gate of the castle was closing. It was getting lower and lower. The children ran as fast as they could.

Chip ran to the gate and rolled under it.

"Come on!" he shouted. "We don't want to be shut out of the castle."

They got under the gate just in time. Then it shut with a loud clang.

Biff didn't like the adventure much. It was hard work.

"It's not fair," she said. "This is Nadim's adventure and he's not even here."

The children came to three doors. They didn't
know which one to open.

"I think we should go through this one," said
Wilf. "It looks like a keyhole."

He pushed the door and it began to open.

"Come on, let's go through," he said.

The door shut and they found themselves in a room full of mirrors. Each mirror made them look a funny shape.

In one mirror they looked fat and round. In another they looked long and thin. In another they had funny-shaped heads.

The mirrors made them look so funny that they all laughed and laughed.

"I've got an enormous head and a little, thin body," laughed Wilf.

"I hope we don't go on looking like this," said Chip. "Think what Mum and Dad would say."

The children went into the maze. Soon they
came to a dead end.

"I think we went wrong at the last turning,"
said Biff. "We'll have to go back."

Wilf remembered the monster's map.

"I think I know which way to go," he said.
"Follow me."

The children came to a hall with squares on the
floor. Some of the squares had numbers on them.

There was a doorway at the end of the hall,
but it was high up in the wall.

"How do we get up to that door?" asked Kipper.

"I wish Nadim was here," said Biff. "He'd know."

Biff was right. The square lifted the children
up to the door in the wall.

Chip looked at the floor.

"I see," he said. "All the squares add up to
fifteen whichever way you cross them. Only one
way adds up to six."

"Mind you don't fall," said Biff.

They came to a new room. A nasty-looking
robot began to come towards them.

"Help," called Kipper. "It's going to get us."

The robot came closer.

"That's funny," said Chip. "It's just like one
of Nadim's toys."

Suddenly, Chip began to laugh.

"I'm not frightened of this robot," he said.

"Come on, everyone," he called. "Help me to push."

He ran up to the robot and gave it a push. The others helped. The top of the robot began to open.

"Look who's inside," shouted Kipper.

Nadim was sitting inside the robot.

"That was clever of you, Chip," he said. "How did you know I was inside here?"

"Because you wrote a story about this robot at school," said Chip.

"Well done, Chip," said everyone.

The magic key glowed and the adventure was over. Nadim was sorry. "It was fun being the Master of Storm Castle," he said.

"We had to go through the castle and you didn't," said Biff. "You can put your computer away, and we'll have a game of football."